The 10-Step Action Guide to Completing What You Started:

Develop Self-Discipline, Take Action and Execute your Goal

Quawsi Samuel

Table of Contents

Introduction 4
1. Be Selective in What Projects You Consider Doing 6
2. Estimate the Resources You Need 8
3. Budget Your Energy and Timeline Accordingly 10
4. Quit Being a Perfectionist 12
5. Commit To It 14
6. Connect with Your End Vision 17
7. Follow the Path of Highest Enjoyment 20
8. Track Your Progress 22
9. Celebrate What You've Done So Far 24
10. Don't Force It If It's Really Not Working Out 26

Introduction

Do you have a tendency to start various projects, but never finish them?

Are you good at starting a project and setting a goal, but never reaching completion?

If so, you are not alone.

I was at that point too, and many people have a habit of starting projects and not finishing them. This is a bad practice in life.

Completing a project can easy, but it takes proper planning and genuine action skills. If you have ever embarked on a project, then you know that every project comes with its own set of challenges. Some of those challenges may not be clear when you first start.

I have embarked on many projects for my profession, my business, and in pursuing my personal goals. As a result, I have a wealth of experience when it comes to taking projects from beginning to end. This 10-step action guide is aimed at helping you reach your goals.

Completing your goals effectively all starts with employing the following acronym: S.M.A.R.T.

- Specific
- Measurable
- Attainable
- Realistic
- Time-bound

It should be simple to understand what it takes to complete the task. The required measures should be sensible, and the task should have a certain level of significance. Your goal should not be set too high or too low, but should challenge you. In other words, it should be a little over what you think you can actually do. Once all these attributes are present, anyone undertaking that project should be off to an excellent start.

1. Be Selective in What Projects You Consider Doing

When you begin a project, make sure you are passionate about seeing it through to completion. This is especially true for large projects. Completing the task must be part of your motivation.

I realized that I had not completed projects in the past because I had little or no interest in them. By engaging in those projects, I realized that I wasted a lot of time. I could have spent that time engaging in something that I was a bit more passionate about. My time would have been better utilized.

If you are interested in your goal, your rate of completion will be much higher. If you are not sure that you will be able to complete a large-scale project, then break it down into five to ten phases. After completing the first phase, ask yourself if you still want to continue.

Action step Challenge #1

Write list of project/Goals that you are passionate about completing

2. Estimate the Resources You Need

To be successful in achieving your goals, it's important to have all the resources you need. You don't want to realize this half-way through your project.

Resource planning can help prepare you for complex projects. In this type of planning, you would estimate how many resources are needed for the entire project. Afterward, you can plan out the cost and the manpower needed to execute the project.

That means creating a quick plan on how much effort and time your idea will take. This gives you an eagle's eye view of the overall picture. It doesn't have to be comprehensive; just a simple outline will help. The main point of this exercise is to have something to guide you.

Action step Challenge #2

For each goal listed in Challenge #1 write down everything that you will realistically need to finish the project/Goal

3. Budget Your Energy and Timeline Accordingly

To complete what you started, it is essential that you budget your energy and time. After you create your outline, pursue a realistic idea of how much time and effort is necessary to complete your task. Calculate your timeline and plan how the resources will be used. Integrate that into your to-do list. Set aside time in your calendar for the project. Give yourself some lag time as well in case of delay for one reason or another.

Working with people, I found that the major reason why people get demotivated is because they underestimated the amount of work involved. This is why budgeting time and energy is important. It actually makes a person focus on the details necessary to complete the project. Once you know that you have to put in a certain amount of time and work to get the final result, you will manage yourself to achieve your target. This leads to a higher success rate.

Action step Challenge #3

For each project or goal listed in Challenge #1, clearly state how much energy you have to put into the project for it to be a success and also calculate the total timeframe the project can take to complete.

4. Quit Being a Perfectionist

This is a major contributor for many of my projects not getting past the starting line. Many of us have a subconscious habit delaying work because we want to make sure it's just right. I have had my fair share of incomplete projects because I was spending too much time tweaking everything to make sure it was perfect. After several failures, I realized that a goal does not have to be done perfectly to be successful.

I understand the idea of perfectionism, and I believe in pursuing it, but not to the point of hindering you from achieving your goals. Consider setting a threshold that you are willing to accept, and a timeframe you can embrace to achieve your goals.

As a result, some goals may call for you to challenge your inner perfectionist when necessary. Consider doing a sort of rough draft version of the goal. Then pick up the fine details later by setting secondary goals. The main idea is to get it completed.

Action step Challenge #4

Before engaging in a project, write down specific threshold in which you are willing to accept for you to move forward and also set individual timeline for each task that you can reasonable accept to move forward.

5. Commit To It

For a project to reach the stage of completion, there must be some level of commitment. It's important that once you start a project, you commit to it. Whatever you plan to do, do it. If the plan is not in alignment with your ultimate goal, then you may need to review and adjust your plan. Otherwise, hold steady to your word and honor it.

For example, I had to produce a newsletter once that was set for completion on the last day of the month. I made a commitment to the executive team that I was working with at the time. Although I could have requested an extension and enjoyed some sightseeing, I decided to honor my original commitment.

I wanted the regular readers of that newsletter to receive it on time. Going to the beach or sightseeing was something I could always do another time.

Ask yourself what's important to you when you are committing to your goals and deadlines? Is it going to an event for the weekend or working on that business you have always dreamt of setting up?

The first option might bring you some temporary satisfaction, but the latter is what truly gives you fulfillment. By choosing the second option, you can reap the benefits for a much longer period.

Action step Challenge #5

Write task list of all the items you have to get done and the date for completion and be determined to complete each task according to plan.

6. Connect with Your End Vision

To stay motivated, and achieve the goal you set out to do, you should stay connected to your end vision.

Many times when we start a task, we start off hyped and ready to take massive action on anything that comes our way. Once we get into the core parts of the project, it's like all the hype and energy fade away. You find yourself losing interest in continuing the project.

You may still be excited about the overall goal, but you are not fascinated by the smaller tasks that are essential for you to complete it.

At this point, you must realize that every bit of the puzzle now counts toward realizing your end vision. The main problem here is your end vision has become disconnected from you. You just need to be able to visualize your vision once again to get back on track.

Surround yourself with anything that prompts you to think of your end goal, such as a vision board. Include pictures that represent the goal and people who have achieved the same goal.

Action step Challenge #6

Take note of some things that will keep you motivated during the project. You can start by listing some of the reasons for starting the project

7. Follow the Path of Highest Enjoyment

I have realized the simple way to finish my projects is to be open-minded and flexible toward my approach. For example, most people will complete their to-do list in sequential order. I did this for a period in my life until I came to the firm realization that it was not the most effective approach.

Some days, I procrastinate on the first task because I might be more interested in the third task. Being flexible means that you can still be productive even on the days you are not performing at your highest potential. When you are flexible, you can work on the task at hand while maintaining the boundaries of the project.

In conclusion, you must create proper rules for the project that fit your criteria. Don't just follow a method that is working well for another person. When you become flexible on the path that you create, you automatically become productive in your work.

Action step Challenge #7

Map out a pathway of the project you will enjoy for every task that you are doing for in the overall project. For this challenge you can brainstorm the most convenient alternative to get the job complete.

8. Track Your Progress

Like the previous steps, tracking your progress helps in understanding what you've accomplished and how much you have left to do. It makes completing your goal much easier because you are keeping up with the momentum of the project at hand.

Develop a project log that records the current status and targets for your project. Clearly define the target of the goal. For example, if your goal is to lose or gain twenty pounds in six months, then your weekly log can show your progression as you proceed to your ultimate goal.

By keeping a log, you may realize after three months that you have only gained or lost three pounds. At that point, you will know that you have to change your approach to make your goal for the next three months. This is important because it makes you accountable and helps you stay on the right track.

Action step Challenge #8

Create a record of the all the tasks that you have completed during the process

9. Celebrate What You've Done So Far

Many times, we get demotivated with the multitude of things that need to be done. It can be overwhelming sometimes. It seems like for every ten steps we take forward, there are always a thousand more to go. It can seem impossible to finish. Sometimes the magnitude of the task engulfs us, and we are ready to quit halfway through the project.

One thing we should be mindful of is to celebrate what we have accomplished so far. The fact that you have already started the process toward your goal is a major accomplishment because many people never start. In reality, you wouldn't celebrate each task in a significant way, but you can create milestones. At these intervals, you are able to rest, recharge, and regroup. Then you can celebrate what you have done so far before continuing.

Action step Challenge #9

Write down a set predetermine milestone points in the project at which you will choose to celebrate your achievement so far. You can also write down what you will do to celebrate

10. Don't Force It If It's Really Not Working Out

Sometimes you may lose the desire to complete a certain goal. It happens, but don't give up. It's a normal part of the process.

Remember, change is constant. We change, our interests change, and sometimes even our ideas and plans change. The faster you are aware that something is not working out, then the faster you are able to move forward.

When you reach the point where you can't continue, consider reevaluating your goals. Check to see if the two versions align. There may be necessary elements of the previous goal that might be relevant to the new one.

I adopt the transitional approach to goals that aren't working out. You will realize that instead of abandoning projects midway through, you could be embracing those projects. For example, let's say that I started writing several articles without completing them. After developing a transitional approach, I realized that many of the incomplete articles could still be utilized. I was still able to use the content as I transitioned from an old project to a new one. Give yourself the consent to drop the things that are not working. You might be surprised to see many new things coming your way right after making that decision.

Action step Challenge #10

Identify some risky areas of the project that may cause the project to fail and for each area listed, create a contingency plan for those areas

Notes

Notes

Notes

Notes

Notes

Resources

https://www.inc.com/jeff-haden/7-habits-of-people-with-remarkable-mental-toughness.html

https://www.inc.com/peter-economy/5-powerful-ways-to-boost-your-confidence.html

https://www.entrepreneur.com/slideshow/299836

http://www.uncommonhelp.me/articles/self-discipline-techniques/

http://blog.iqmatrix.com/self-discipline

https://www.wanderlustworker.com/how-to-discipline-yourself-with-10-habits/

http://www.uncommonhelp.me/articles/self-discipline-techniques/

www.ingramcontent.com/pod-product-compliance
Lightning Source LLC
Chambersburg PA
CBHW030044230526
45472CB00005B/1662